BE AN EFFECTIVE COMMUNICATOR

SOCIAL NETWORKING

HAYLEY NORRIS

ROSEN PUBLISHING

NEW YORK

Published in 2022 by The Rosen Publishing Group, Inc.
29 East 21st Street, New York, NY 10010

Copyright © 2022 by The Rosen Publishing Group, Inc.

First Edition

Portions of this work were originally authored by Jared Meyer and published as *Making Friends: The Art of Social Networking in Life and Online*. All new material in this edition was authored by Hayley Norris.

All rights reserved. No part of this book may be reproduced in any form without permission in writing from the publisher, except by a reviewer.

Library of Congress Cataloging-in-Publication Data

Names: Norris, Hayley, author.
Title: Social networking / Hayley Norris.
Description: New York : Rosen Publishing, [2022] | Series: Be an effective communicator | Includes bibliographical references and index.
Identifiers: LCCN 2021031843 (print) | LCCN 2021031844 (ebook) | ISBN 9781499470291 (library binding) | ISBN 9781499470284 (paperback) | ISBN 9781499470307 (ebook)
Subjects: LCSH: Social networks--Juvenile literature. | Interpersonal relations--Juvenile literature. | Friendship--Juvenile literature.
Classification: LCC HM741 .N67 2022 (print) | LCC HM741 (ebook) | DDC --dc2302.302853
LC record available at https://lccn.loc.gov/2021031843
LC ebook record available at https://lccn.loc.gov/2021031844

Manufactured in the United States of America

Some of the images in this book illustrate individuals who are models. The depictions do not imply actual situations or events.

CPSIA Compliance Information: Batch #CWRYA22. For further information contact Rosen Publishing, New York, New York at 1-800-237-9932.

CONTENTS

INTRODUCTION — 4

CHAPTER 1
FORMING FRIENDSHIPS — 7

CHAPTER 2
INGREDIENTS FOR GREAT RELATIONSHIPS — 19

CHAPTER 3
STRENGTHENING YOUR FRIENDSHIPS — 33

CHAPTER 4
KEEPING UP WITH YOUR FRIENDS — 45

CHAPTER 5
BUILDING RELATIONSHIPS FOR LIFE — 59

GLOSSARY — 70

FOR MORE INFORMATION — 72

FOR FURTHER READING — 74

INDEX — 76

INTRODUCTION

With cell phones, social media, and other modern technologies right at the tips of our fingers, communicating has never been easier—but it's also never been more complicated. As long as humans have been alive, they've been cultivating relationships. Today, the internet allows people all over the world to connect and get to know each other. This creates opportunities to meet likeminded people one might otherwise never cross paths with. It also brings people with vastly different views together.

Some people find online friendships to be satisfying and rewarding. However, socializing with people online will always be different than socializing with people face-to-face. In face-to-face friendships, you can truly share your life with people and you can communicate with them in all sorts of ways. With online friendships, communication may be limited to texting or messaging, and while these can be fast and easy ways to communicate, they can also be complicated and limiting. Words sometimes lose their meaning when expressed strictly through text. However, many people enjoying sharing content, such

Social media websites are also sometimes known as social networks. Social networking has come to be associated with people communicating online, but it really just means creating and maintaining relationships, online or in person.

as memes and funny videos, with their friends across the internet.

Social media websites and apps, such as Instagram, Twitter, Facebook, and TikTok, are great ways to communicate with friends. But social networking is actually about much more than just the relationships we have with our friends. It is also about learning new things and can even involve forming professional and academic

SOCIAL NETWORKING

relationships. Social networking opens people to thoughts and opinions of people they may otherwise never hear from. In this way, social networking can help shape a person's worldview.

Of course, whether you're talking to someone online or in person, safety is always important. You should never give out personal information to a stranger. Even if you think you've gotten to know someone, you should not give your personal information out over the internet. Additionally, social media websites and apps often have age restrictions and other rules. This is for your own safety. You should always follow a social media website's rules.

Whether online or in person, developing good relationships is an important key to success. You probably already have lots of meaningful relationships in your life, from family and friends to teachers and coaches. Social networking is a tool you can use to find even more.

CHAPTER 1
FORMING FRIENDSHIPS

When you think of your closest friendships, you can probably think of at least a few benefits that have come out of those relationships. Fun experiences and companionship are probably things you've gained from friendships. You may have also learned new things from a friend, met new people, or been exposed to new opportunities. Perhaps a good friend has listened to your feelings or helped you through a difficult time. And perhaps you've done the same for them. Being there for someone can feel good, and it can benefit both yourself and the other person.

You may be familiar with the expression "you can never have too many friends." However, it's also often said that quality is more important than quantity. It's easy to see that the more connections you have, the less you're able to give everyone an equal share of your time, effort, and focus. The less available you are, the more likely that some of the relationships you maintain won't be as strong as others. Given the amount of time we have in our daily lives, some of our relationships may be more like acquaintances than close friendships. Many people think it's better to have a few great friends than many acquaintances. That doesn't mean, however, that there aren't benefits to knowing lots of people. After all, that's what social networking is all about.

The overall experience of making friends will be easier to manage and enjoy when you completely understand a few fundamental aspects of friendship. In this chapter, we'll explore some ways to prepare and protect yourself when connecting with new people.

MANY FORMS OF FRIENDSHIP

If you were to categorize making friends like a school subject, it would be more of an art than a science. Maintaining friendships is an art too. There is no one official way to approach friendships. Rather, different types of friendships and relationships fall over a wide spectrum On one end of the spectrum may be people you met just once and haven't connected with since. On the other end of the spectrum may be people with whom you have shared consistent, strong, lifelong friendships. These may be the friendships you've had for many years, perhaps since you were a child. Scattered throughout the spectrum, you may find childhood friends whom you have known since you were younger. You may or may not currently be in contact with them. If you do keep in touch, you may not currently be considered very close. Close friends may be thought of as those with whom you consistently keep in touch. These may be the friends whom you care about more than others.

Your best friends may be those people with whom you are currently the closest and share your life experiences with the most. Alternatively, acquaintances may be people you

With today's technology, you may be in nearly constant contact with your best friends.

have met only once or twice and with whom you have an inconsistent relationship. These are the type of people who would likely be pretty easy to reach if for any reason you wanted to connect with them. However, even though you could reach them, acquaintances are often people you'd more likely run into by chance. They could be friends of friends and you may have a nice time with them occasionally, but you would not consider them part of your main friend group. Finally, connections may be those people whom you've met once and have rarely, barely, or never connected with since the first time you met. A great thing about connections and acquaintances is that there is the potential for them to become closer friends. But even if they never do, there can still be benefits to these types of relationships.

Each friendship can have unique components such as when you met, how you met, how long you've been friends, how close you are,

FORMING FRIENDSHIPS

Close friendships are usually the most meaningful, but there are benefits to having acquaintances and connections too. They can help you meet more friends or find important opportunities.

Connecting Online in Hard Times

While the most meaningful relationships usually involve some in-person contact, there are also lots of benefits to connecting with people online. The COVID-19 pandemic made this clearer than ever. Schools and businesses all over the world shut down in 2020 and into 2021 in an effort to stop the spread of COVID-19. When this happened, many people began going to school online or working from home. For many people, these changes were difficult at first. They missed the daily connections that happen when you go into a building with the same classmates or coworkers every day. However, certain tools helped people adjust. Thanks to the technology available today, people were able to maintain their connections with friends and acquaintances.

Remote learning allowed for students to keep up with their studies during the COVID-19 pandemic. It was also a way for them to keep up with friends and classmates when they couldn't meet in person.

FORMING FRIENDSHIPS

Videoconferencing websites such as Zoom became especially important for maintaining relationships during the COVID-19 pandemic. Classrooms and meetings turned virtual. Since it wasn't safe to see friends in person, many set up times to meet and chat over Zoom or other videoconferencing platforms. Even though it wasn't the same as seeing your friends in person, it helped people maintain the connections that were important to them. Other groups, such as clubs and fitness classes, also turned virtual. There were even platforms that allowed people to join together for movie or game nights. These apps let friends watch a movie at the same time or play a game together while also talking through chat boxes or videos. While this wasn't quite the same as being able to get together with friends in person, it kept friendships alive and allowed for people to continue social networking in a safe way.

how often you communicate, and how you share experiences together. Therefore, the term "best friend" may mean something different to you than it does to another person. The shared experiences and length of time you've known another person often form the foundation for the type of relationship that you have with someone.

MAKING NEW CONNECTIONS

Given the popularity of the internet and social media, which includes websites and apps such as Instagram, Twitter,

TikTok, and Facebook, practically anyone with an internet connection and basic computer skills can make friends online. People can make friends at any time of the day or night from practically anywhere in the world. Making friends online might seem more convenient than making friends in person. However, there's nothing quite like meeting new people face-to-face. Meeting people in the flesh offers a more personal and complete experience. Such an experience leads people to enjoy higher levels of satisfaction both personally and socially.

There are several differences between meeting friends online and making friends face-to-face. Making friends in real life allows you to quickly judge a person's character by his or her behavior. It also helps you evaluate how a person treats you and others. It even allows you to see for yourself if the other person is able to communicate naturally in person. This is because you're sharing a part of your lives together and not just an electronic communication. Online communication can sometimes be edited and crafted to sound just right. Talking in person, however, is more personal and natural.

Compared to meeting in person, there are usually limitations to connecting with someone online. For example, there's only so much you can share online. Often, only text, images, and videos can be shared between two people over the internet. Using videoconferencing, or video-chat, platforms such as FaceTime, Zoom, or Skype, can be beneficial to keep up with friends when it's difficult to do so in person, but you should not video-chat with strangers. If you have developed a friendship with someone you met online, you should be honest and open about it with your parent or guardian. They can help you decide if it is safe to continue communicating with them.

SAFETY FIRST

Would you be more likely to trust someone you met in person or someone you met online? Sometimes meeting people online provides less certainty about their real personality, true identity, and real intentions. Upon meeting people online, you may never be able to verify their true identity, especially when they don't live in the same area as you. Just as you'd never share private information with someone you just met in person, you should never share private information with someone you met online.

You may never know if the new friends that you make on social media sites such as Instagram or TikTok are truly who they say they are. Of course, this may eventually be proved by sharing more interactions and communications. Still, you may never really know what a person is truly like if you don't meet them in person. That is certainly not to say that you should meet people you have spoken to only online in person. In fact, you should never do that unless you've discussed it with your guardian and they either accompany you or give permission for another trusted adult to accompany you. Even still, this type of meeting should only ever be done in a very public setting. Whether you meet someone online or in person, they may not always turn out to be

SOCIAL NETWORKING

If you've only spoken to someone online, they could be anyone. Make sure a trusted adult knows about anyone you connect with online.

FORMING FRIENDSHIPS

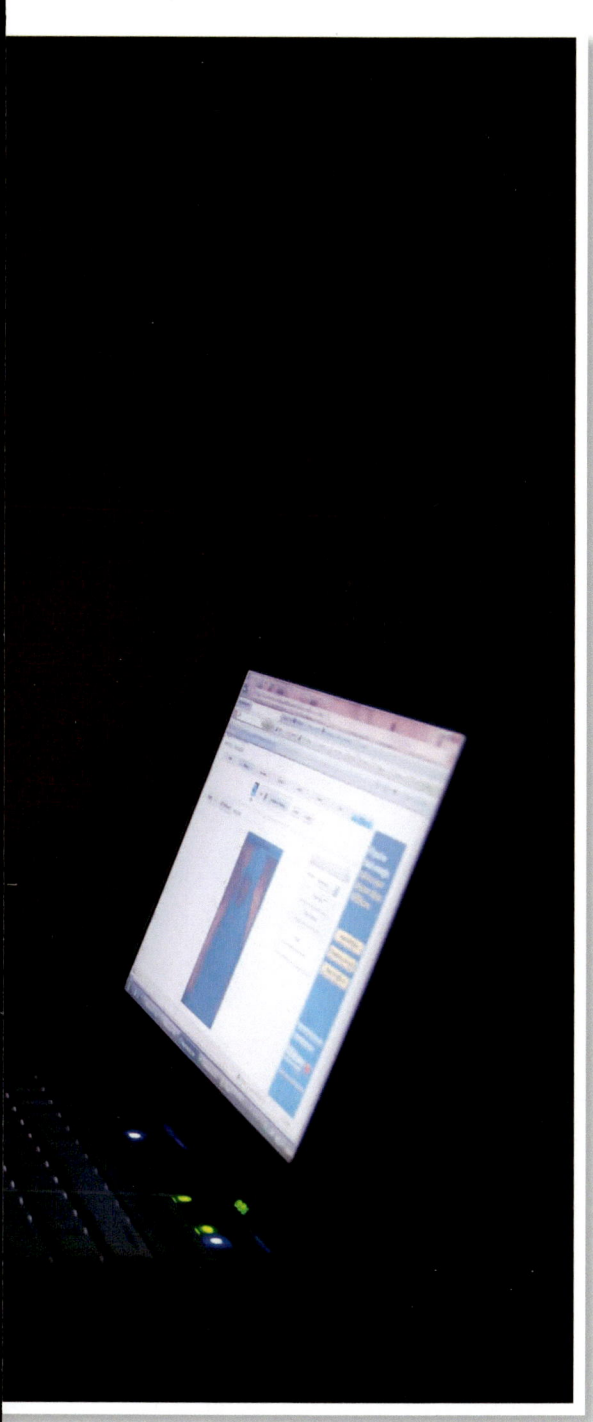

who you expect them to be, and it's important to always keep your safety in mind.

DIFFERENCES BETWEEN FRIENDS

The more you can relate to someone that you've recently met, the more likely it is that you'll want to be friends with them. However, people with very different personalities can still have great friendships. What people need to understand when it comes to making friends with others that have vastly different personalities is that no two people will ever be exactly alike. People are unique and they will often see, want, and do things differently. Additionally, people have different priorities. Their personal lives, schedules, and obligations to other people will be pretty different. And yet, most people are still not only able to get along but also share some great friendships with people very dissimilar to themselves.

Setting expectations about making friends that are realistic will make getting along with different people easier. If everyone were exactly like you, you'd probably get bored pretty quickly. Despite people's basic personality differences, two friends with very different and even conflicting beliefs, values, and goals can still get along well and have a great time together. What's their secret? The more fundamental values related to friendship that they share, the more likely they will be able to build a great friendship. For example, two people might come from completely different backgrounds. They might be part of different communities, political parties, religions, or have or want totally different careers. But if they both believe friends should always be honest with each other and be able to laugh at themselves, then these two very different people might still make very good friends. You never know who could be a good friend if you don't give them a chance!

CHAPTER 2

INGREDIENTS FOR GREAT RELATIONSHIPS

Today, social networking has come to be associated with people connecting online. However, at its core, social networking just means creating and maintaining relationships. You can social network online or offline. Depending on your personality, you might find it easy or difficult to make friends. But whether you connect with new people easily or not, you can find opportunities to meet new people and make new friends.

For kids and teens, school is usually the most common place to make friends. You might make friends with the person who sits next to you in math class or someone

SOCIAL NETWORKING

who lives in your neighborhood and rides the same bus to school as you. Often, these kinds of friendships form naturally, but even if they don't, there are other ways to make friends. Joining a club, sports team, or other extracurricular activity often results in meaningful friendships. Common

Being part of a sports team or other group can help you make friends naturally. If you all like soccer, you already have something in common to talk about off the field.

INGREDIENTS FOR GREAT RELATIONSHIPS

interests often bring people together and can act as the glue that holds a relationship together.

If you put yourself out there, you could meet new people every day. However, taking such an intensive approach can be overwhelming. This is especially true when you attempt to manage more relationships than you can handle. That's particularly hard to do while tending to other priorities and obligations in your life. Such an approach is clearly not for everyone. Some people find it a bit scary to meet or talk to new people. Even though spending time in person tends to be the best way to get to know someone, some people might find it easier to chat by texting with someone they've just met. There's no one right way to make friends.

When meeting new people, there are two factors over which we have little or any control: chemistry and compatibility. These are two powerful components to relationships that can rarely be faked or forced. Without these two basic but important ingredients, the likelihood of a friendship forming is fairly low. In the first chapter, you learned that understanding the fundamentals of friendship prepares people to get along with new friends. This chapter will cover a few important aspects of connecting with new people for the very first time as well as during your first few interactions.

PERSONAL CHEMISTRY.

Have you ever met someone and you just immediately feel comfortable with them? The conversation comes easy and you feel like you're on the same wavelength. Maybe you have a similar sense of humor and are quickly laughing together. That's chemistry. Two people with a strong amount of personal chemistry often just "get" each other. It is the one ingredient that can either make or break a new connection. Additionally, there is no specific formula for how much chemistry two people need in order to motivate them to develop a friendship. Upon meeting, two people will often be able to tell if they're interested in building something deeper with one another based on their initial interactions.

Some people believe that chemistry can't develop over time like its counterpart, compatibility. They may prefer not to keep in touch with another person if the connection isn't strong enough from the very start. Other people may believe that chemistry between two people can evolve over time. They believe that they may get along better at some point in the future. And so, they may become better acquainted at another timedown the line. Either way, it always comes down to a personal choice: do you choose to invest in new relationships with people with whom you have remarkable

INGREDIENTS FOR GREAT RELATIONSHIPS

You can't make personal chemistry in a lab, but you can connect with your classmates! Being paired together for a school project is one way people can learn they have something in common and become friends.

chemistry, or do you try to make things work with practically anyone with whom you think you could be friends?

ARE WE COMPATIBLE?

Compatibility is based on how many things you have in common with someone else, whether they are perceptions, preferences, or even priorities. Often, the more you have in common with someone, the more likely you are to relate to them. However, you can still be compatible with someone who sees, wants, likes, and does things very differently than you.

Unlike chemistry, compatibility is more likely to evolve over time. In fact, it may take just one or two changes in people's lives to allow them to relate more or better to someone that they know. While our fundamental personalities rarely change over the course of our lives, we usually have the ability to make both minor and major modifications here and there to our behavior. Any number of changes to one's perceptions, preferences, and priorities can bring two people closer. Alternatively, if one friend's personality changes dramatically, it may pull the two people apart.

If you feel like you have to completely change who you are to be someone's friend, however, they might not be a good friend for you. There is a big difference between small changes, such as trying to be on time more often so your friend doesn't have to wait for you, and big changes, like quitting a club you enjoy because your friend doesn't like it. A true friend will appreciate you for who you already are and shouldn't ask you to make any dramatic changes to your personality. Likewise, you shouldn't expect anyone to change who they are to be more compatible with you. Some people simply aren't compatible, and that's okay.

While the supply of people that you can become friends with is abundant, strong chemistry between two people is typically rare. This is because chemistry is the unique result of two personalities making a great match. Still, if there is compatibility there is at least a basis for friendship, and great chemistry, at least initially, is not always needed for friendships to develop.

THE THREE C'S

A few extremely attractive traits that help people make friends and good first impressions are a healthy level of confidence, the capability of being cooperative, and, not surprisingly, great communication skills. These three things—confidence, cooperation, and communication—encourage people to share a decent initial interaction and possibly move toward developing a new friendship.

Having a healthy level of confidence is very attractive to people because it shows that you're self-secure. This also allows them to assume that you're content with who you are and where you are in your life. Furthermore, confidence also often conveys that you have a strong, resilient personality. Confident people are more often protected from uncomfortable things like personal criticism or even fear and doubt. However, it is possible to seem overly confident or arrogant. Bragging is usually considered a turnoff to most people. You can be modest in conversation and still appear confident.

But what if you just don't feel confident sometimes? That's okay, and it happens to everyone. We all have days when we just don't feel our best. At these times, some people live by the phrase "fake it till you make it," meaning if you act confident, even if you really don't feel that way, you

First Impressions

You may have heard the expression, "you never get a second chance to make a good first impression." As obvious as it sounds, this phrase emphasizes the fact that people may make firm judgments about you based on your behavior and appearance during your very first interaction with them.

Making a good first impression can help you make friends, just as a good first impression from someone else can make you want to be their friend. As you grow older, however, you may realize that sometimes your first impressions are actually wrong. Maybe the person you met just received some bad news or wasn't feeling well. Your first impression of them might have been that they are withdrawn, irritable, or simply not fun to be around. You might decide right away that they're not someone you want to be friends with. But if you've ever been in a bad mood, you can likely attest to the fact that the way you act when you're in such a mood is not the way you act the majority of the time. So, yes, first impressions are important, but they're not always completely accurate, and it's best to try to keep an open mind. After all, would you want someone to judge you based solely on your worst day?

Some of the best friendships have happened because one person gave the other a second chance. Even if a second chance proves that your first impression was right, you can at least know you tried. Maybe the experience will help you learn how to better deal with similar situations in the future. You might even realize that while the person probably won't ever be a best friend, they might be a nice acquaintance or connection to have.

INGREDIENTS FOR GREAT RELATIONSHIPS

will likely come off as confident and perhaps even start to feel that way.

It's easy to be friends with people you easily get along with. You may meet some fantastic people whom you'd love to get to know better. What may quickly change your mind, however, is when you start to recognize the signs that it would probably be difficult (and even sometimes near impossible) to be friends with them. This may be due to their unique personality and uncooperative nature. People like others who aren't overly demanding and are simply nice to be around. If someone has no interest cooperating with you, they likely wouldn't make a very good friend, and if you aren't cooperative, people will likely assume the same about you.

Communication is considered by many people to be the foundation of good relationships. Without healthy communication, you've got nothing more than someone in the same room as you. Having such a companion can be like not having a companion at all. The better your companion is at communicating, the easier it will be to develop a friendship with them. This includes both written and verbal communication. Whether you approach someone at a party to start a conversation or send someone an initial text message, what you say and how you say it matters.

APPROACHABILITY, AUTHENTICITY, AND INQUISITIVENESS

We've learned that being confident and cooperative while being able to communicate effectively is important when meeting new people and trying to establish new friendships. Assuming you've got a good level of chemistry with someone you've just met and that you have a few things in common, there are three more traits that most people find very appealing in new friends. These are approachability, authenticity, and inquisitiveness.

If you were to meet someone who had their arms crossed and was frowning, you may not immediately be interested in starting a conversation with them. Because of their body language, they may not seem approachable. Approachability is another word for appearing friendly. When you appear open to talking to other people, you allow others to approach you, whether it's to start a conversation about the book you're holding or even to ask you for the time. Such a light approach to starting a conversation allows two people to make an initial connection and establish a good rapport. This allows them to feel each other out and decide whether they want to get to know each other better. However, it's important to realize that just because someone doesn't appear approachable, it doesn't necessarily mean they aren't friendly. For example, some people think not making eye contact makes a person seem uninterested or unapproachable. However, some people just have difficulty making eye contact. It doesn't mean they aren't nice or don't want to be your friend. This is yet another reason you shouldn't judge people too quickly.

How compatible two people are is usually based on how much they can identify and relate to each other. This is normally and naturally done by considering one's own identity and comparing it to another's. When two people who have just met act naturally and behave as normally as they would in any other social environment, they can tell that their conversation and intentions are authentic. Being authentic means being genuine. This is easy to do when you're secure with who you are and relatively comfortable being vulnerable when connecting with someone new. Some people, however, do fake their authenticity. This is especially easy for people to do online, when they're hiding behind a computer screen. This is one reason it's important to always keep your safety in mind and never give out personal information.

Having a healthy dose of curiosity, or inquisitiveness, is a good trait to have when meeting someone new. Without being curious about people you've just met, it's often difficult to get to know them unless they're naturally an open and assertive communicator. If they're not particularly open (or even curious) themselves, the conversation could quickly come to an end. This may prove that one or both of you has difficulty meeting new people or that one of you is simply not interested in talking further.

One of the easiest ways to show people that you're genuinely interested in getting to know them is by asking questions. Authentic, appropriate questions that allow you to share an enjoyable conversation may lead to future conversation. Asking questions also allows you to learn about their background, interests, goals, and even values. The more open you are to being asked questions, the easier it will be to get to know you, too. However, it's important to make sure you're not asking invasive questions. For

SOCIAL NETWORKING

When meeting someone, asking questions is a great way to get a person talking, even if they're typically shy around new people.

INGREDIENTS FOR GREAT RELATIONSHIPS

example, you can ask someone you're just getting to know what sports they like to play, but you should not ask them what their address is. Of course, this is something that might come up down the road, for example if you develop a friendship with them and are invited over to their house, but it is not the kind of thing you should usually ask when you've just met someone. This is because information such as one's address is personal information. Likewise, if someone you have just met is asking you invasive questions, you should not answer them and should tell a trusted adult.

MYTHS and facts

MYTH
The best relationships are easy.

FACT
In a perfect world, everyone would always get along and enjoy each other's company. This would make relationships pretty easy. In reality, though, there's no simple approach to having great, long-lasting relationships. Some relationships take a lot of work but are still worth it to both people.

MYTH
It's best to have a lot of friends.

FACT
You can never have too many connections, but good friendships require time and effort. No one has unlimited time, and putting effort into too many friendships can be tiring and even make some friendships weaker. It's often better to have a few great friendships than many just-okay friendships.

MYTH
The older you get, the harder it is to make new friends.

FACT
Since school is such a common place for young people to make friends, some people do find it more difficult to make friends when they are adults (and no longer go to school) as compared to when they were in school. However, with effort it is always possible to make new friends. The more experience a person has attempting to build new relationships, the easier it becomes to meet and relate to new people. Friendships can come and go, and while many people may still have strong, lifelong friendships later on in their lives, there will always be new opportunities to make new friends. For example, joining groups or clubs based on interests can help people of any age make new friends.

STRENGTHENING YOUR FRIENDSHIPS

You've probably experienced friendships that are different than others. Maybe you have a friend you talk to at school, but you don't see each other outside of school. Meanwhile, you might have another friend with whom you spend lots of time outside of school. Perhaps you have a friend at summer camp that you spend all summer with, but then you don't see them for the next 10 months. When you're back together, though, everything is normal and it's like you never missed a beat. All of these friendships can be important. They can all be strong and meaningful. This is because all friendships are different.

Not all friendships are as strong as others, however. A friendship can become as

SOCIAL NETWORKING

strong as both friends want it to become. The relationship can become stronger slowly over time or grow quickly over a relatively short period. When you first meet someone, you may not know what's in store as far as where your relationship with them will go. Maybe you will become best friends right away, or maybe the other person will not be interested in a new friendship at the moment. You may meet people

Even if you keep up with your friends from summer camp online or on the phone during the school year, there's nothing quite like being back with them in person!

STRENGTHENING YOUR FRIENDSHIPS

and communicate with them inconsistently during the next month or so. However, a few months or even years down the line, you may eventually become great friends.

Skills for stronger friendships, such as teamwork, keeping commitments, and generosity, are important during the beginning stages of meeting someone new. They are usually even more important, however, as the friendship develops over time. In fact, these are just a few things that not only bring two people closer but also prove to one another that their relationship is important.

So far you've learned about the fundamentals of friendship and the basics of meeting new people. This chapter will review a few additional skills that you can use to develop much stronger relationships with your new friends and hone in on your social networking skills.

ON THE SAME TEAM

A friendship can be very much like a team. The two team members have a shared goal as well as a personal stake in the progress, experiences, and outcomes of their relatively small group. When you approach friendships like they are teams, it helps remind you to

35

behave as if the friendship is never just about you. It also reaffirms that you're not the only one who benefits from the relationship. Furthermore, it reminds you that you're also not the only one who has something to lose. Like any team of which you're a member, the more time and effort that you contribute to the group, the more valuable it will become. This is why the longer you have a friendship with someone, the more special it will be and the more you will trust each other.

Trustworthiness is determined by how reliable and honest you think someone is in a friendship. When it comes to trust, the longer you and your friends have had a relationship, the deeper the level of trust you share will be. And so, it's very rare that people will trust each other very much upon meeting for the first time. In fact, it's very common that they may not trust each other at all. This is perfectly normal because trust is usually earned and experienced over time. One of the fastest ways to develop trust is to try and find out about a person's past. There are no guarantees that someone's previous actions will predict their future behaviors. However, it's good to know if someone has a history of being dishonest or untrustworthy. You would probably like to find out sooner rather than later if your new friend may not be trustworthy with regard to specific things such as keeping secrets or borrowing money. Once again, the internet can make things even more complicated in this regard. Trustworthiness can be quite difficult—or sometimes nearly impossible—to determine when you are only talking to

STRENGTHENING YOUR FRIENDSHIPS

someone through texting or social media. It's important to have a network of friends you know in person so that you can truly develop trust with the people in your life.

Developing trust with a new friend can begin quickly when you are introduced to them by another friend. Furthermore,

You many not always get along with friends of friends, but meeting people through others is one way to ensure you'll at least have something in common.

anytime throughout the friendship, you could always ask the friend you have in common about your new friend's trustworthiness. This could be about anything from sharing private information to sharing personal property. Another benefit of meeting friends through other friends is that you can develop a larger circle of friends to hang out with together.

FOLLOW THROUGH

One component of developing trust in a relationship is one's willingness and ability to keep commitments. A commitment is a thing a person agrees to do, such as an event you promise to go to with a friend at a specific time and place. You can also make a commitment not to do something, such as a promise to never drink and drive. There are less serious commitments too, such as committing to wait to see a certain movie until your friend can see it with you. No matter how serious a commitment seems, keeping commitments is one of the most important aspects of a friendship.

Priorities and obligations change throughout our lives, and sometimes we have to change or even cancel our commitments. This might require a difficult conversation with your friend, such as telling them you can no longer go to the baseball game you promised you'd attend with them because you forgot it was at the same time as a family gathering. Most friendships can survive some situations like this. However, if a consistent pattern forms where a person in the friendship has difficulty keeping commitments, the quality

STRENGTHENING YOUR FRIENDSHIPS

If you've ever had to wait around for someone who is late or doesn't show, you probably know it doesn't feel great. Good communication can help everyone get along.

of the relationship will most likely suffer. If too many commitments are broken over a relatively short period of time, it may be difficult to regain the trust that has been lost.

Discussing personal preferences in a friendship is one of the ways you can lay the groundwork for the rest of your relationship. The sooner two people communicate their preferences with regard to the type of friendship they want, the sooner disappointment can be prevented. While you may think you can tell how flexible someone is by thinking about their general nature, it's always smarter to ask rather than assume.

When it comes to making commitments such as meeting up with a friend at a particular time, people can always at least try to accommodate their friends' lifestyles and personalities. This is where compromising comes into play. Let's say that you're usually laid-back and often a bit late to appointments. Your friend, however, is more rigid and perhaps starts to worry if you are even a minute late. You can both still work out a way to make plans to get together without causing anyone stress or disappointment. In this case, for example, you could make a deal with your friend that if you are running late you will call or text them to let them know. If you know you can stick to it, you could also tell them that you will not be more than five minutes late. When you set a specific time to meet someone, you should always try to be on time, but sometimes being a bit late is unavoidable. Once you're able to set reasonable expectations, you can usually make appropriate arrangements and maintain a relatively harmonious friendship.

Balancing Friendships

Too many friendships can be tough to maintain. One reason for this is that sharing is such a big part of friendship. Whether you're sharing your time, games, or snacks, too many people to share with can mean no one gets enough of anything. There's only so much we're capable of giving to people. No one can be everything to everyone. There's also only so much we can do within a normal day. The more friends you have, the more time and effort you have to put into the friendships. Just like having a relatively well-balanced life is healthy, so is having a manageable number of friendships. How many friends a person has is a personal choice. Since we can't share everything with everybody, having just a few friends may be both easier and more satisfying to you.

Some friendships may be more focused on one person than the other. Other friendships may be perfectly balanced where each contributes an equal amount of things to the relationship. Because generosity and sharing take so many forms, it may be impossible to determine if two friends share equally and fairly. For example, it's pretty hard to compare the value of four small favors in one week to one big gift during the same month. When something like sharing doesn't seem or feel right, bring it up during your next conversation with your friend. You'll probably figure out the concern pretty quickly and know what changes your friendship may need. If one person is clearly putting more into the friendship than the other, it could mean the friendship means more to them, or it could mean that the other person is balancing too many other friendships. It could also be a misunderstanding. But you can't figure it out if you don't talk about it!

SOCIAL NETWORKING

Remember, friendship itself is a gift. Some people prefer to simply spend quality time with a friend rather than giving or receiving gifts. Sharing and giving should not always be about material items. In fact, if a friendship were just about giving and receiving material things, it wouldn't be a very strong friendship at all. Sharing your feelings with a friend, giving them a listening ear when they're having a hard time, or simply sharing time together are excellent ways you can be generous with your friends.

KEEPING UP WITH YOUR FRIENDS

It's rare for a great friendship to form overnight—or even within days of meeting someone. Excellent friendships usually form naturally and can take any amount of time to form, whether it is over a few days or over many months or years. Sometimes, the people involved don't even realize that a friendship has formed until it has already happened.

In some instances, two close friends might not feel exactly the same way about each other. One friend might say the other is their only best friend, while the other might say they have multiple best friends. Either way, if it's a great friendship and

SOCIAL NETWORKING

Large friendship groups often create nice communities, but it's normal to have one or two friends in the group you're closest with.

the two people involved are really close, there's no need to stress yourself out over grouping your friends into categories like "best friend" or "closest friend." Sometimes you just know what you've got with someone and categorizing it won't really make a difference. When this happens,

KEEPING UP WITH YOUR FRIENDS

you know you've got a pretty amazing friendship. It doesn't matter whether you choose to label someone as your "best friend" or not.

One's closest friends are usually considered the most important friends in their life, but what is it that causes best friends to have such amazing relationships? There are many factors, but the more you care about someone, the more likely you'll consciously try to invest in your friendship and prevent conflict. This chapter covers a few important ways to express how much you value your friends when you interact with them in person or online. It also covers important skills that often lead people to become amazing friends.

HONESTY: THE BEST POLICY

The longer you know someone, the easier it usually is to be honest and direct with them. Being honest and direct with people you don't know very well can sometimes be difficult. Not everyone will agree with your opinions. When people hear opinions they don't agree with, they may quickly become defensive or even angry in order to protect themselves from criticism.

This is especially common with online communication, where people can say anything they want without the fear of in-person conflict.

Even among your closest friends, there may be opinions that some in the group don't agree with. But there are ways to communicate these thoughts without hurting feelings. If you're good friends with people, it would only make sense that you should be comfortable sharing your honest thoughts with them. Hopefully, you'd also appreciate receiving the truth in return. When being honest about something you know your friend might not like, it's important to be tactful and not simply criticize or complain. It's not just what you say that matters, but also how you say it.

BE CONSIDERATE

While it's safe to assume that friends will treat each other well most of the time, sometimes one of you may accidentally do or say something hurtful. If you know your friends well, you'll probably be able to tell what type of comments or actions will likely be considered offensive or hurtful to them. Still, it's sometimes easy to lose control when you're playing around or even poking some fun at good friends. It's important to remember to try to make positive contributions to a friendship. If you do unintentionally say or do something hurtful to a friend, you should apologize. It can also be helpful to have a conversation with the friend about what was said. If you didn't realize what you said or did was hurtful, having a talk about it can help you better understand their feelings and avoid hurting them in the future. A good friend should be open to doing the same for you if they accidentally say or do something hurtful.

Being considerate is easy to do when you remember that your friendship is a team where each member considers the other's needs and wants as much as their own. Sure, sending a thank-you note can be considered thoughtful and considerate after a friend does something special for you. Yet there are so many more creative ways to be considerate in return. Being considerate usually proves to people that you're not taking them for granted, since you're doing or saying something that shows that you value them.

A quick way to size up a friendship is to evaluate how much appreciation, consideration, and effort you both contribute to the relationship. The more you and your friend appreciate each other, are considerate of each other's needs and wants, and make an effort to maintain a friendship, the better chance your relationship will last well into the future.

SHOWING GRATITUDE

Saying "thank you" is a pretty standard practice that usually comes naturally to people. Beyond having the good manners that most people would expect of you, being appreciative or showing gratitude toward your friends can be really easy to do. How often do you hear friends say how much they appreciate having you in their lives? How often do you hear them tell you what they admire about you? It may be difficult for some people to share such gratitude with others.

Being appreciative may make them feel vulnerable. Therefore, they may feel that not saying anything prevents them from possibly getting rejected. Alternatively, sharing one's appreciation may also bring friends closer, and this may be something a friend may not be comfortable doing. The fact remains, however, that people (especially those in friendships) crave appreciation and approval. Being told you're important through a text or online message might feel nice, but hearing a close friend say the words aloud and to your face can feel amazing. Don't just assume your friends know how you feel—tell them! Gratitude helps friendships flourish, especially when it's shared.

CHANGING FRIENDSHIPS

The health of a friendship can change at any time. Sometimes it may be exciting, sometimes it may just exist, and at other times it may be exhausted. A friendship may even be on the verge of ending. What you and your friends contribute to your friendship today will determine where it ends up tomorrow. Friendships blossom each time effort is made between friends. The higher the quality of contributions that each of you contributes, the healthier and stronger a friendship will be. However, it's natural for a bond between two friends to fluctuate and change over time.

KEEPING UP WITH YOUR FRIENDS

It's normal for some friendships to end. If it feels like all your friendships are ending though, it might be helpful to speak to someone, such as a counselor, to figure out how to better form and maintain friendships.

Again, because making friends is more of an art than it is a science, there is no perfect formula for maintaining a perfect relationship.

Loving Your Friends

When it comes to friendships, people have different styles or ways of caring for and appreciating their friends. It's normal to care differently about different friends. There are some friends you may care about deeply, while there are other friends you may not care about nearly as much. But if they are truly your friend, you will probably care about them on some level. Friendship is based on love, and the love you have for a friend is the result of how much compassion and care you feel toward them.

Compassion is another word for sympathy. It has to do with the concern and regard you feel about another person's situation or circumstances. Imagine a friend of yours is suffering from a minor illness like a cold, or something much worse like a close family member dying. How you react to the news can quickly tell you how you feel about and relate to the issue. Additionally, what you say, and especially how you empathize with your friend, can say a lot about you. It will reflect your personality, how you relate to your friend, and how much the friend means to you.

Some people are more emotional than others. Others may be considered less caring. There are also people who may come across as too caring. If someone seems too caring, it may seem fake or like they are just pretending to care. There's no perfect way to feel or behave when you learn that a friend is dealing with a difficult issue or life event. You don't need to struggle with how you feel about hearing bad news. Some people are resilient to most unfortunate circumstances, whereas others may need emotional support during rough times. What's most important is that you be a supportive friend.

BONDING THROUGH UNDERSTANDING

Your friends won't always do things the same way you would. Likewise, the way you do certain things might surprise or even shock some of your friends. Knowing when and how to understand, accept, and forgive friends can help prevent conflict and guide you in building even stronger friendships.

Being understanding doesn't necessarily mean that you will always know why a friend does or says something differently than you would. It simply means being able to fully recognize that you and your friend are unique individuals. Also, it means that while you may have some or even many things in common, you both will still have many significant differences. When it comes to making plans with friends, for example, one friend may prefer to call on the phone whereas another may prefer to text. When you completely understand that your friends have perceptions, preferences, and priorities that are often different from yours, it's so much easier to get along with them.

ACCEPTING FRIENDS FOR WHO THEY ARE

There are a lot of things that happen in life and friendships that we can't control. When things happen that we would rather not have experienced, it can be frustrating to deal with the consequences. Learning to allow your friends to be

SOCIAL NETWORKING

You may have friends who do not get along with each other. You can keep being friends with both of them. You may just have to accept that they are different people and spend time with them separately.

KEEPING UP WITH YOUR FRIENDS

themselves can help keep the friendship strong. It also takes the pressure off of you to resist or even change your friends. Your friends are going to make mistakes, say the wrong things, do silly things, or even do things that you could do or have done so much better. While many people enjoy the power of personal development, it's often better to accept your friends for who they are rather than try to change them and make them become someone else. Besides, it's easier to help someone change when they truly want to make personal changes in their life. Just because you think things would be easier or better if your friend changed something in their life doesn't make it true. As long as they are not hurting themselves or others, it is usually best to accept your friend's differences or quirks and to simply love your friend for who they are.

FORGIVENESS

Even with the people you love the most, it can be difficult to forgive wrongdoings. Whether a friend knowingly or accidentally said or did something to hurt you, forgiveness is important if you want to keep the friendship alive and well. Being forgiving means completely releasing any concerns, criticism, disappointment, and anger related to a specific action, event, or experience for which someone is directly responsible. In order to forgive friends for something they did that upset you, simply telling them you forgive them will probably not make much of a difference in how you feel about it. Even if you believe it to be true, it probably won't be enough.

True forgiveness takes place by completely releasing resentful thoughts when you talk about the issue with your friends. You don't have to request that they change. You don't even need to request an apology. It's highly suggested, however, that to truly forgive your friends, you tell them in person that you forgive them and why. Otherwise, you may hold hidden resentment and anger toward them. Completely forgiving someone can seem difficult, but you can laugh about it even while doing it. Forgiveness can be one of the hardest parts of friendship. Before telling a friend you forgive them, it might be helpful to first have a conversation about the thing they did or said that hurt you. They may not even be aware that they did something wrong and, in that case, just telling them you forgive them could seem passive-aggressive or might make them angry. When trying to move past any conflict, it's important for both friends to understand why the conflict exists. Even if you disagree whether what happened was right or wrong, understanding each other's points of view can help avoid such conflicts in the future, and can allow the person who feels wronged to more genuinely forgive their friend. In turn, these events can lead to even stronger bonds between friends.

SOCIAL NETWORKING

10 Great Questions TO ASK A GUIDANCE COUNSELOR

1. Why are we not formally taught how to make friends or build relationships in school?

2. What are some icebreakers that I can use to get to know others?

3. What are a few easy ways for a new student to make friends at school?

4. Is there a club at school to help new students make friends? If not, can I start one?

5. What do you think are a few good reasons to start making new friends?

6. What do you think is the secret to lifelong friendships?

7. Do adults usually have an easier or harder time making new friends?

8. Why do some friends randomly disappear from our lives?

9. Do you suggest pursuing a new friendship with someone who's known for being difficult?

10. How can people build confidence and protect themselves from experiencing rejection from friends or potential friends?

BUILDING RELATIONSHIPS FOR LIFE

New friends can be made at any point during one's life—whether it's during school or college, at work, during retirement, or even later in life. With social media, it's also easier than ever to find old friends and rekindle relationships that may have ended. Since there will always be new friends to make, the ones you've known the longest may be even more important to you.

Today, with the internet, social media, and cell phones, the potential for communication is nearly always at our fingertips. This can certainly help strengthen friendships and make it easier to connect with friends more often. However, by making it easier to maintain many less meaningful friendships, it may weaken stronger friendships.

While there now are more opportunities to make new friends than ever, there are also plenty of opportunities to replace even our newest friends. New friends are great, but there is something different about lifelong friendships. It can be fulfilling just knowing someone for many years. It can also be even more special when you've shared a consistent friendship and many memories throughout that time. Being loyal and treating your most valued friends like they're family members are two ways to ensure that the friendship flourishes. The more you naturally want to treat friends like they're family members, the more likely you'll be connected for life. In this chapter, we will discuss the very special nature of lifelong friendships.

SHARED MEMORIES

Friendships come in all shapes and sizes. Today, you may have some good friends whom you may not see again until a few years from now. For some, it's possible you may never speak with them again. Alternatively, you may make friends tomorrow whom you will know and care about well into your retirement years. There is usually a profound connection between two people with shared experiences spanning a good portion of their lives.

Most people find that the older they get, the more they cherish the friendships they have with friends they've had the longest. They may also deeply appreciate the friendships they still have with friends they might have been closer with when they were younger, even if they are not as close anymore. No matter how many close friends you have and no matter how consistent those friendships may be, you may remain connected in some way in the future.

Making new friends can be wonderful. However, the feeling of sharing memories with an old friend hardly compares to having just met someone yesterday. The more experiences friends share, the richer their relationship can become. Friends who meet face-to-face and build their friendship in person will more likely have a deeper connection. They can still share and communicate online, but having the opportunity to share experiences together will bring them closer.

There are so many differences between having friends in life compared to having friends online. People have the freedom to enjoy both general types of friends. However, there's nothing quite like being in the same room with a friend and experiencing the same thrilling, scary, or even mundane things together. What makes only having online friends less satisfying than having friends in life is that there are limitations on what online friendships can offer. You can share content and communication online, but what about everything else you do in your life?

Life can be busy, and when even your closest friends' priorities and lives change, the friendship may lose its strength and momentum. Both friends may decide to focus on and invest more toward other relationships. They can still remain connected online with the option of revitalizing

SOCIAL NETWORKING

When you've known someone for most or all of your life, you share memories with them that you can't share with anyone else.

the relationship in the future. Friendships can come and go. They can also still mean something special to two old friends when they reunite after years of being totally disconnected.

TOGETHER THROUGH CHANGE

As teenagers or adults, two great friends who have known each other since kindergarten may not have as much in common as they did while growing up. However their shared history, similar interests, and similar senses of humor can still make being friends fun. But what happens when one of them goes off to college or moves across the country? It's possible that the friendship could suffer from such

SOCIAL NETWORKING

The End of a Friendship

We mentioned earlier that sometimes friendships end. Often, this happens naturally, with both friends slowly drifting apart from each other. There may not have been any particular event that caused them to stop being friends, they just become less close over time. Other times, one person might realize that the friendship is no longer (or never was) very healthy or beneficial for them. There are lots of reasons this may happen. Maybe one friend feels taken advantage of or left out of a group situation. Maybe one friend betrayed the other's trust or did something that the other person isn't ready to forgive.

It can be hard to end a friendship, but sometimes it is what's best for both people. It is, however, important for both people to remain respectful of each other. If you're considering ending a friendship, it may be worth having a chat with the person. Perhaps there was a misunderstanding, and the friendship can be mended. This isn't always the case though. When a friendship ends, there is no need to be mean or try to turn other people against the old friend. It's often important to keep an amicable relationship with old friends, especially if you go to the same school or may have other reasons to see each other in person in the future. While the person may no longer be a good friend for you, they might remain a worthwhile acquaintance or connection. Maybe sometime in the future you will even be friends again.

big life changes. Even the best friendships in life can evolve into completely online friendships, or the friends could lose touch for good.

One of the easiest ways to prevent the loss of a friendship is to be a consistent friend. Doing this is simple when you make a consistent effort to maintain your relationship. You can do this even if you're thousands of miles apart and don't have constant access to the internet. If you value the friendship enough, you'll still want to proactively be part of your friend's life. But what happens if your friend isn't interested? As previously mentioned, nothing is guaranteed when it comes to friendships. That's what makes having best and longtime friends so special.

FRIENDS BECOME FAMILY.

One of the benefits of having family members is the likelihood that they will be some of the few people with whom you'll have the longest history. Another benefit is the commitment that family members share with each other. While friendships can come and go, the relationships people have with their families are more likely to last because of their special bond. Imagine if you could combine the benefits of having a family with the benefits of having friends. While you may never live together, approaching your friendships from a position of being like family may make your relationships even stronger.

Many times, when conflicts come up within families, they are committed to working out their challenges, even if it is

SOCIAL NETWORKING

Your closest friends might be so comfortable with you that they are also friendly with your family. They might regularly join you at family get togethers.

BUILDING RELATIONSHIPS FOR LIFE

difficult. When problems come up within friendships, however, they may only be resolved if both parties feel that the relationship is worth the effort. Unlike family members, friends can eventually, easily, and often be replaced.

Treating your friends like they're family members is more likely to occur further down the line when the friendship is very strong and very important to you. In longer friendships, it's possible that this can happen naturally. One day, you may realize you feel very similarly toward your best friend as you do toward your brother or sister. The benefits of treating your friends like they're family include knowing

SOCIAL NETWORKING

> Social networking can lead to some of the most rewarding and special relationships in your life!

that you will both likely be willing to work things out during hard times and that you have a friend with whom you may very likely be close for the rest of your life.

Social networking involves making and maintaining all types of relationships throughout your entire life. The most meaningful of these relationships will likely be the ones with your best or closest friends. These are the people whom you can trust, be honest with, and truly share your life with.

GLOSSARY

academic Having to do with school or education.

acquaintance A person someone knows but is not very close with.

amicable Showing politeness and avoiding conflict.

authenticity The ability to be one's true self.

compatibility The ability for people to be friends harmoniously without conflict.

component A part that helps make up a whole.

cooperation Working together in harmony.

cultivating To develop or improve something through careful attention.

empathize To share the feelings of another person.

fundamental Of or relating to the primary principle on which something is based.

harmonious Showing and being in agreement and not fighting.

intensive Vigorous in nature.

meme An amusing item, such as a humorously captioned picture or video, that is spread widely online, often through the use of social media.

misconstrue To interpret something incorrectly.

opportunity A chance to do something.

pandemic An outbreak of a disease that occurs over a wide geographic area.

passive-aggressive Behavior characterized by the expression of negative feelings, resentment, and aggression in a non-active way.

profound Very intense.

resentful The state of feeling or being bitter for having been treated unfairly.

revitalizing Giving something new life, energy, or strength.

spectrum A continuous range of something.

verge An edge or border.

vulnerable Open to attack or harm.

FOR MORE INFORMATION

Alumni Channel
1124 Greenbriar Rd.
Cherry Hill, NJ 08034
(609) 379-3580
Website: www.alumnichannel.com
Alumni Channel is an organization that offers alumni groups an easy way to get organized, keep active, and grow. The services it provides are great for people starting an alumni group or those who already have an organization set up and running.

Friendship Force International
279 W. Crogan Street
Lawrenceville, GA 30046 (404) 522-9490
Website: www.thefriendshipforce.org
Friendship Force International promotes friendship as well as goodwill by supporting travel exchange programs. Friendship Force has clubs in more than 60 countries around the world.

The Girl Scout Network
Girl Scouts of the USA
420 Fifth Avenue
New York, NY 10018
(212) 852-5055
Website: www.girlscouts.org/en/adults/the-girl-scout-network.html
The Girl Scout Network is part of Girl Scouts of the United States of America and offers opportunities for former Girl Scouts to reconnect and stay connected, as well as to make new friends through various types of events.

Girls Inc.
120 Wall Street, 18th Floor
New York, NY 10005
(212) 509-2000
Website: girlsinc.org
Girls Inc. is devoted to the development of the next generation of female leaders, and its mission includes fostering the development of strong interpersonal communication skills in young women and giving young women mentors who will actively listen to them.

National Communication Association
1765 N Street NW
Washington, DC 20036
(202) 464-4622
Website: www.natcom.org
The National Communication Association studies all forms, modes, and consequences of communication.

National 4-H Council
7100 Connecticut Avenue
Chevy Chase, MD 20815
(301) 961-2800
Website: www.4-h.org
This organization provides opportunities for young people to network and make new connections and offers programs to help develop practical skills and leadership capabilities.

FOR FURTHER READING

Byron, Paul. *Digital Media, Friendship and Cultures of Care.* New York, NY: Routledge, Taylor & Francis Group, 2021.

Covey, Sean. *The 7 Habits of Highly Effective Teens.* New York, NY: Simon & Schuster, 2014.

DiPiazza, Francesca, *Friend Me!: 600 Years of Social Networking in America.* Minneapolis, MN: Twenty-First Century Books, 2012.

Fitzsimons, Kate. *The Teen's Guide to Social Skills: Practical Advice for Building Empathy, Self-Esteem, & Confidence.* Emeryville, CA: Rockridge Press, 2021.

Folger, Joseph P., Marshall Scott Poole, and Randall K. Stutman. *Working Through Conflict: Strategies for Relationships, Groups, and Organizations.* New York, NY: Routledge, 2021.

Ford, Jeanne Marie. *Respecting Opposing Viewpoints.* New York, NY: Cavendish Square Publishing, 2018.

Hurley, Katie. *A Year of Positive Thinking for Teens: Daily Motivation to Beat Stress, Inspire Happiness, and Achieve Your Goals.* Emeryville, CA: Rockridge Press, 2020.

Hurt, Avery Elizabeth. *Coping with Political Disagreements among Friends and Family.* New York, NY: Rosen Publishing, 2019.

Koya, Lena. *Networking Women: Building Social and Professional Connections.* New York, NY: Rosen Publishing, 2017.

Kuromiya, Jun. *The Future of Communication.* Minneapolis, MN: Lerner Publications, 2021.

Lombardo, Jennifer. *Social Networking: Staying Safe in the Online World.* New York, NY: Lucent Press, 2017.

MacCutcheon, Megan. *The Ultimate Self-Esteem Workbook for Teens: Overcome Insecurity, Defeat Your Inner Critic, and Live Confidently.* Emeryville, CA: Rockridge Press, 2019.

Randy, Charles. *Communication Skills.* Broomall, PA: Mason Crest, 2019.

Skeen, Michelle. *Communication Skills for Teens: How to Listen, Express & Connect for Success.* Oakland, CA: Instant Help Books, 2016.

Vengoechea, Ximena. *Listen Like You Mean It: Reclaiming the Lost Art of True Connection.* New York, NY: Penguin Random House LLC, 2021.

INDEX

A

acceptance, 53, 54, 55, 56
acquaintances, 8, 9, 10, 11, 12, 26, 64
approachability, 27, 28
authenticity, 27, 28, 29

B

best friends, 9, 13, 26, 34, 45, 46, 47, 65, 67
body language, 28

C

cell phones, 4, 53, 59
  calling, 40, 53
  text messaging, 4, 14, 21, 27, 37, 40, 43, 53
chemistry, 21, 22, 23, 24, 25, 28
clubs, 13, 20, 24, 32, 58
college, 59, 63
commitments, 35, 38, 40, 65
common interests, 20, 21
communication, 4, 13, 14, 15, 25, 27, 29, 35, 39, 40, 43, 48, 59, 61
  face-to-face (or in-person), 4, 5, 6, 12, 13, 14, 15, 17, 21, 34, 37, 42, 47, 48, 51, 56, 61, 64
  online, 4, 5, 6, 12, 13, 14, 15, 16, 18, 29, 34, 42, 43, 47, 48, 50, 61, 65
compassion, 52
compatibility, 21, 22, 23, 24, 25, 28
compromising, 40
confidence, 25, 27, 58
conflict, 18, 47, 48, 53, 57, 65
connections, 8, 10, 11, 12, 13, 14, 22, 26, 28, 32, 60, 61, 64
consideration, 48, 49
cooperation, 25, 27
counselors, 51, 58
COVID-19 pandemic, 12, 13

D

differences, 4, 14, 17, 18, 24, 52, 53, 56
disagreements, 47, 48, 57

E

empathy, 52
ending friendships, 64
eye contact, 28

F

family, 6, 52, 60, 65, 66, 67
favors, 41, 42
first impressions, 25, 26
forgiveness, 53, 56, 57, 64
friend groups, 10, 35, 36, 46, 48
friendship spectrum, 8, 9

G

generosity, 35, 41, 42, 43, 44
gift giving, 41, 42, 43
gratitude, 49, 50

H

honesty, 15, 18, 36, 47, 48, 69

I

icebreakers, 58
inquisitiveness, 27, 28, 29, 31

J

jokes, 42, 43

K

keeping in touch, 9, 12, 14, 22, 34, 44, 45

L

lifelong friendships, 9, 32, 58, 60, 69

M

memes, 5, 42
memories, 60, 61, 62
misunderstandings, 41, 64

N

new friends, 15, 19, 22, 25, 27, 28, 32, 34, 35, 36, 37, 38, 58, 59, 60

O

obligations, 18, 21, 38
online friendships, 4, 6, 14, 15, 42, 61, 65
online messaging, 50

P

personal information, 6, 29, 31
personalities, 15, 17, 18, 19, 24, 25, 27, 40, 52
personal lives, 18
preferences, 23, 24, 40, 42, 53
priorities, 17, 18, 21, 23, 24, 38, 53, 61

Q

questions, 29, 30, 31, 58

R

reconnecting with old friends, 59, 63
rejection, 50, 58
remote learning, 12, 13

S

safety, 6, 13, 15, 17, 29
school, 8, 12, 19, 20, 23, 32, 33, 34, 58, 59, 64
sharing, 4, 8, 9, 13, 14, 15, 18, 38, 41, 42, 43, 44, 48, 50, 61, 62
socializing, 4
social media, 4, 5, 6, 13, 14, 15, 37, 59
   Facebook, 5, 14
   Instagram, 5, 14, 15
   TikTok, 5, 14, 15
   Twitter, 5, 14
sports, 20, 31
summer camp, 33, 34

T

teamwork, 35, 36, 49
timeliness, 24, 39, 40
tone, 43
trust, 15, 36, 37, 38, 40, 64, 69

U

understanding, 42, 43, 49, 53, 57

V

videoconferencing, 13, 14, 15
   FaceTime, 14
   Skype, 14
   Zoom, 13, 14
videos, 5, 14, 42
vulnerability, 29, 50

PHOTO CREDITS

Cover Flamingo Images/Shutterstock.com; p. 5 Rido/Shutterstock.com; p. 9 Bricolage/Shutterstock.com; pp. 10-11, 30-31, 46-47, 66-67 Monkey Business Images/Shutterstock.com; p. 12 insta_photos/Shutterstock.com; pp. 16-17 Shannon Wine/Shutterstock.com; pp. 20-21 Rittis/Shutterstock.com; p. 23 Air Images/Shutterstock.com; pp. 34-35 Vikulin/Shutterstock.com; p. 37 inewsfoto/Shutterstock.com; p. 39 leungchopan/Shutterstock.com; p. 51 VH-studio/Shutterstock.com; pp. 54-55 Bojan Milinkov/Shutterstock.com; pp. 62-63 wavebreakmedia/Shutterstock.com; p. 68 Makistock/Shutterstock.com.

Editor: Kate Mikoley
Designer: Michael Flynn